Introducing PL/SQL to SQL Users

Enhance Your SQL with PL/SQL Procedural Logic

- Bundle SQL statements in PL/SQL program
- Complement SQL with PL/SQL procedural logic
- Wrap and reuse PL/SQL program as SQL function
- Store, secure and share PL/SQL program in the database

Djoni Darmawikarta

Table of Contents

Introduction

Introducing PL/SQL to SQL Users is for SQL users who do not have PL/SQL skill.

If you wish you can write some procedural logics in a SQL statement, such as controlling the process flow using IF THEN ELSE logic, you need to consider using PL/SQL.

This book, which introduces PL/SQL basic features, is a perfect starting point.

- You can further learn PL/SQL from my other book, *Oracle PL/SQL Programming Fundamentals – 2nd Edition*.

What is PL/SQL?

PL/SQL partners with SQL.

- PL/SQL is the Oracle procedural language extension of SQL.
- It is integrated within the Oracle database. When you install an Oracle database, PL/SQL is included in the installation.

A PL/ SQL program can have both SQL statement and procedural statement.

- In the program, the SQL statements are used to manipulate **data stored in a database**.
- The procedural statements are used to process data and **control the program flow**, such as using the if-then-else and iterative (looping) structures.

Prerequisite Skill

You (SQL users) should have SQL skill.

- You should be have been writing and executing SQL statements.
- If you ever need to learn, or re-learn, SQL, read my other book, *Oracle SQL*.

Book Examples

To learn the most out of this book, try the book examples.

- Best is to type in the source codes, especially the short ones.
- Execute simply by pressing the Run Script button or F5 on your keyboard.

To practice the examples, you need to have two pieces of software:

- SQL Developer, the GUI IDE (Graphical User Interface Integrated Development Environment) we use to write and run (test) the PL/SQL programs.
- Oracle database Express Edition, where we have the database accessed by the PL/SQL programs.

If you have them on your own computer, you can freely and safely follow the examples.

- You can download them free of charge from the Oracle website.
- The appendix of this book guides you to get and set them up.

The book examples are tested on the Windows version of SQL Developer version 4.1.2.895.

- This was the latest version available from Oracle website at the time of writing this book.
- If you already have a SQL Developer, you can check its version as follows: **Help** > **About**.

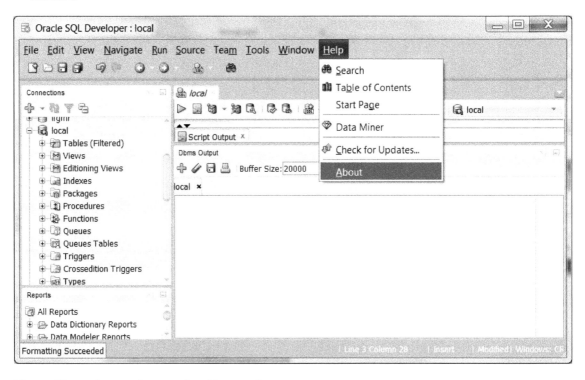

You will see the version on the **About** tab.

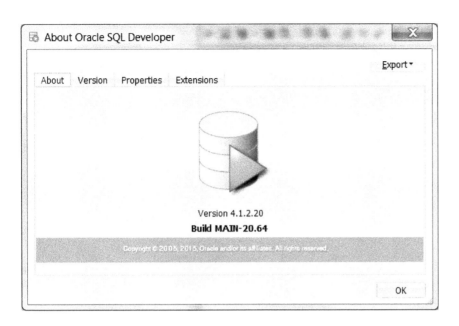

Chapter 1: Introducing PL/SQL

PL/SQL is a block-structured programming language.

- A PL/SQL program consists of one or more blocks.
- A block has three parts: Declaration, Executable and Exception-handling.
- A block has the following structure.

```
DECLARE
  Declaration
BEGIN
  Executable
EXCEPTION
  Exception-handling
END;
```

The three parts of a block are separated by the DECLARE, BEGIN, EXCEPTION, and END PL/SQL reserved words.

- You should not use a reserve word for any other than its designated purpose.

The parts contain statements:

- Declaration statement is for example for declaring a variable.
- Executable statement is for example for executing a SQL statement.
- Exception-handling statement is for example for trapping and handling an error (exception) when no data is returned by a SQL query.

Here's an example program that has the three parts.

- Each part has only one statement. (You can certainly have way more than one statement in any of the parts)
  - The prod_row prod%rowtype means: the prod_row variable is for storing rows having the same column names and data types as the rows of the prod table.
  - A SELECT statement will read the rows of the prod table.
  - The built-in (PL/SQL supplied) no_data_found will handle the exception when no row is returned by the query. The NULL statement, which does nothing, will be executed.
- Each statement must end with a semicolon ;

PL/SQL is not case sensitive

The following program behaves the same and produces the same result as the previous example.

```
declare
    PROD_row PROD%rowtype;
BEGIN
  select * into prod_ROW from prod;
  exception
  WHEN no_data_found then
  null;
END;
```

Only the Executable part is mandatory; the other two parts are optional.

Following our community tradition in programming language introduction, here is our PL/SQL program to display a Hello World greeting.

- The program with only one executable statement (no declaration, no exception-handling) completes successfully.
- Don't forget to open the Dbms Output pane for the connection you're using.
- After you type in the lines of code, run the program by pressing F5.

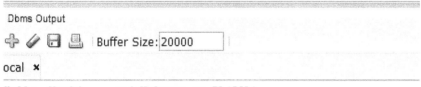

Having learned these PL/SQL basics, you will learn in the next chapter how to bundle multiple SQL statements in a PL/SQL program.

Chapter 2: Bundling SQL Statements

You can have multiple SQL statements in a PL/SQL program. When you run the program, the SQL statements bundled in in the program are submitted altogether to the database server where they will be executed to their completion. Any result (e.g. query output or message) will be responded back to you only when all SQL's execution has been completed.

- Standalone (not inside PL/SQL program) SQL statements are submitted and executed one statement at a time on the database server.
- As a result bundling SQL statements in a PL/SQL program will likely be executed faster than standalone SQL statements.

INSERT, DELETE, UPDATE

The INSERT, DELETE, UPDATE statements are just like you have been using them in a standalone statement.

Here's an example PL/SQL program that uses all of the three statements.

- In this example, we have only one statement of the INSERT, DELETE, and UPDATE statement. In your program, you can include any combination of more than one INSERT/DELETE/UPDATE statement in any sequence.

```
BEGIN
  INSERT INTO prod
    (p_code,p_name, unit_price
    ) VALUES
    (11,'Hammer',11
    );
  DELETE FROM prod WHERE p_code = 22;
  UPDATE prod SET unit_price = unit_price * 1.1 WHERE p_name LIKE
'%Nails%';
END;
```

```
▷ 🗐 🗐 ▾ 🗐 🗟  🗟 🗟  🔍 🗚 ✎ 🗐 🗚    0.062 seconds

Worksheet    Query Builder
   1 ⊟ BEGIN
   2 ⊟   INSERT INTO prod
   3         (p_code,p_name, unit_price
   4         ) VALUES
   5         (11,'Hammer',11
   6         );
   7      DELETE FROM prod WHERE p_code = 22;
   8      UPDATE prod SET unit_price = unit_price * 1.1 WHERE p_name LIKE '%Nail%';
   9    END;
  10

▲▼
🗐 Script Output ×
📌 ✎ 🗐 🖨 🗐    Task completed in 0.062 seconds
PL/SQL procedure successfully completed.
```

SELECT statement

In a PL/SQL program, a SELECT statement (query) is not exactly the same as in a standalone statement.

It must:

- Have the INTO clause.
- Return only one row.
  - If you expect your query will return multiple rows, then you need to use *cursor*. You will learn cursor in Chapter 5: Cursors.

You can have more than one SELECT statement and in combination with any number of INSERT/DELETE/UPDATE statements.

If your SELECT statement is missing the INTO clause, you will get an error shown on the Script Output panel, and the program fails.

```
BEGIN
  SELECT * FROM prod;
END;
```

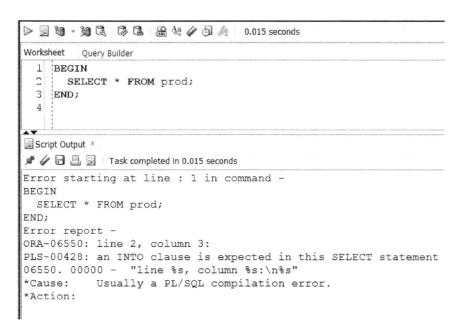

The following query returns more than row hence the error as shown on the Script Output panel.

■ Make sure the PROD table has more than one row before you run the program (F5)

```
DECLARE
  prod_row prod%rowtype;
BEGIN
  SELECT * INTO prod_row FROM prod;
END;
```

```
▷ 🗐 🗐 ▾ 🗐 🗐  🗐 🗐  🗐 🗐 ✎ 🗐 🗐   0.046 seconds
Worksheet   Query Builder
  1 ⊟DECLARE
  2 │   prod_row prod%rowtype;
  3 │BEGIN
  4 │   SELECT * INTO prod_row FROM prod;
  5 │END;
  6 │
```

```
🗐Script Output  ×
📌 ✎ 🗐 🖨 🗐   Task completed in 0.046 seconds
Error starting at line : 1 in command -
DECLARE
  prod_row prod%rowtype;
BEGIN
  SELECT * INTO prod_row FROM prod;
END;
Error report -
ORA-01422: exact fetch returns more than requested number of rows
ORA-06512: at line 4
01422. 00000 -  "exact fetch returns more than requested number of rows"
*Cause:    The number specified in exact fetch is less than the rows returned.
*Action:   Rewrite the query or change number of rows requested
```

SQL statement in Exception-handling part

The following example shows that a program can also have SQL statement in its exception-handling part.

- The example has two SQL statements in its Exception-handling part.

```
DECLARE
  prod_row prod%rowtype;
BEGIN
  SELECT * INTO prod_row FROM prod;
EXCEPTION
WHEN too_many_rows THEN
  SELECT * INTO prod_row FROM prod WHERE rownum <2;
  UPDATE prod SET unit_price = unit_price + 1 WHERE prod_cd =
prod_row.prod_cd;
END;
```

The two rows of prod table are …

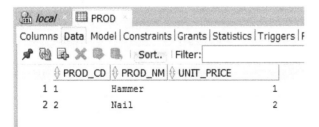

```
🗐 local   🗐 PROD
Columns Data Model │Constraints │Grants│Statistics│Triggers│F
📌 🗐 🗐 ✗ 🗐 🗐   Sort..  Filter:
       ◊ PROD_CD │◊ PROD_NM │◊ UNIT_PRICE
  1 1         Hammer                 1
  2 2         Nail                   2
```

When you run the program:

- The error (exception) caused by the multiple rows returned is handled; the program runs to its completion (does not fail)
- The unit_price of the selected row (happens to be the Nail) is now its original plus 1, which is 2.

Chapter 3: Procedural Logic

You can control the execution flow of a program by adding procedural logic, e.g. the IF …
THEN … ELSE statement.

IF THEN

In the following example:

- The IF … THEN procedural logic checks the number of rows affected.
- The SQL%rowcount, a built-in attribute (supplied by PL/SQL), contains the number of rows affected by its previously executed SQL statement; the UPDATE statement. As the prod table has two rows, the SQL%rowcount will be 2.
- The ROLLBACK statement is executed only if the SQL%rowcount is greater than 1. Note that IF … THEN must be terminated by END IF;

```
BEGIN
  UPDATE prod SET unit_price = unit_price + 1 WHERE unit_price < 2;
  dbms_output.put_line(SQL%rowcount);
  IF sql%rowcount > 1 THEN
    ROLLBACK;
  END IF;
END;
```

Note that a program can have more than one IF THEN and they can be nested (an IF THEN can be within another IF THEN)

IF THEN ELSE

The next example shows the use of the IF THEN ELSE.

- If the average of the updated price is larger than 1.5, then the updated is rolled back (cancelled); else the update is committed (confirmed in the database)
- A program can have more than one IF THEN ELSE and they can be nested.

```
DECLARE
  price_avg NUMBER;
BEGIN
  UPDATE prod SET unit_price = unit_price + 1 WHERE unit_price < 2;
  SELECT AVG(unit_price) INTO price_avg FROM prod ;
  dbms_output.put_line(price_avg);
  IF price_avg > 1.5 THEN
    ROLLBACK;
  ELSE
    COMMIT;
  END IF;
END;
```

Variable and Assignment

We must declare a variable, in the Declaration part, before we can use it in the Executable and Exception-handling parts. In PL/SQL program you use variable to store program data.

- In the previous example, we declared price_avg variable.
  - In the Executable, the SELECT statement stores (assigns) the averaged unit price into the variable.
- The price_avg variable has a NUMBER data type for numeric data.
  - Other data types frequently used are: INT (for storing integer), CHAR (for fixed length character string), VARCHAR2 (for variable length string), and DATE.

In the following example, we also declare reduced_price variable.

- Its data type is the same as that of the price_avg.
- In the Executable part, reduced_price is assigned the result of price_avg * 0.05.
  - We use the := operator (colon equal-sign) to assign a variable on its left with the value on its right, as in the example.

```
DECLARE
  price_avg NUMBER(6,2);
```

```
  reduced_price price_avg%type;
BEGIN
  UPDATE prod SET unit_price = unit_price + 1 WHERE unit_price < 2;
  SELECT AVG (unit_price) INTO price_avg FROM prod ;
  dbms_output.put_line (price_avg);
  IF price_avg > 1.5 THEN
    ROLLBACK;
    reduced_price := price_avg * 0.05;
    UPDATE prod SET unit_price = reduced_price + 1 WHERE unit_price <
2;
  ELSE
    COMMIT;
  END IF;
END;
```

Chapter 4: Storing Program in the Database

Rather than every time running the lines of code, you can wrap them in as a procedure.

- A stored procedure is a database object, hence you use a CREATE statement.
- You name the procedure, price_upd.
- The declaration part no longer needs the DECLARE reserved word; it is commented in the example below.
- When you execute the CREATE PROCEDURE statement, the program is compiled and stored in the database as indicated by the message on the Script Output; you have not run the program yet. See next section: Executing Stored Procedure.

```
CREATE PROCEDURE price_upd
AS
  --DECLARE
  price_avg NUMBER;
BEGIN
  UPDATE prod SET unit_price = unit_price + 1 WHERE unit_price < 2;
  SELECT AVG (unit_price) INTO price_avg FROM prod ;
  dbms_output.put_line (price_avg);
  IF price_avg > 1.5 THEN
    ROLLBACK;
  ELSE
    COMMIT;
  END IF;
END;
```

```
Worksheet    Query Builder
  1 ⊟ CREATE PROCEDURE price_upd
  2   AS
  3     --DECLARE
  4     price_avg NUMBER;
  5   BEGIN
  6     UPDATE prod SET unit_price = unit_price + 1 WHERE unit_price < 2;
  7     SELECT AVG(unit_price) INTO price_avg FROM prod ;
  8     dbms_output.put_line(price_avg);
  9 ⊟   IF price_avg > 1.5 THEN
 10       ROLLBACK;
 11     ELSE
 12       COMMIT;
 13     END IF;
 14   END;|
 15
```

```
Script Output ×
📌 ✏ 💾 🖨 📄   Task completed in 0.015 seconds

Procedure PRICE_UPD compiled
```

Executing Stored Procedure

You can execute a stored procedure by itself using EXECUTE statement as show in the first example.

```
-- First example
EXECUTE price_upd;
```

Or, within a program's Executable part as shown in the next two examples.

- The second example has the stored procedure alone;
- The third, along with other statements.

```
-- Second example
BEGIN
  price_upd;
END;

-- Third example
DECLARE
  x NUMBER;
BEGIN
  NULL;
  price_upd;
  SELECT AVG(unit_price) INTO x FROM prod;
  dbms_output.put_line(x);
END;
```

Securing and Sharing Stored Procedure

Now that you have the program in the database, you can share it with other users, only with those that have the need. So, first let's see how to secure a stored procedure.

When you create database objects, such as a PL/SQL program, you own it. You must grant the appropriate privileges to other users to use it using the GRANT.

To allow (permit) other users execute your programs, you grant them the EXECUTE privilege on the stored programs.

- The following GRANT allows the two users to use (execute) the price_upd stored procedure.
- The users must exist; otherwise the GRANT will fail and you get an error message.

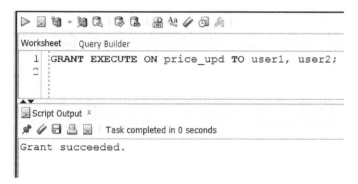

When a user does/should not use a program you revoke the execute privilege.

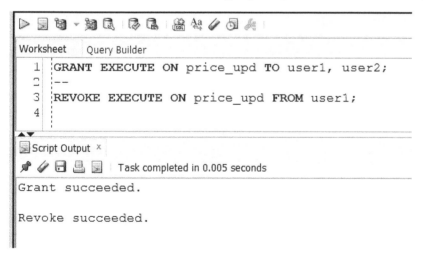

Chapter 5: Cursors

As mentioned in Chapter 2, in PL/SQL you use cursor to handle multiple rows returned by a query.

Stack of rows

A cursor is effectively a stack containing the rows returned by the query.

You use a cursor as follows:

- Declare the cursor. The declaration defines the query.
- You then open the cursor
- Fetch the rows returned by the query one by one sequentially.
- Process each row as necessary.
- Iterate fetching the rows one by one using LOOP.
- To end the loop when there is not any row, use the EXIT WHEN … %notfound.

```
DECLARE
  CURSOR prod_cur
  IS
    SELECT p_name FROM prod;
  name_var prod.p_name%type;
  previous_name_var name_var%type;
BEGIN
  OPEN prod_cur;
  LOOP
    FETCH prod_cur INTO name_var;
    EXIT
  WHEN prod_cur%notfound;
    IF name_var LIKE 'Ham%' THEN
      dbms_output.put_line (name_var);
    ELSE
      NULL;
    END IF;
  END LOOP;
END;
```

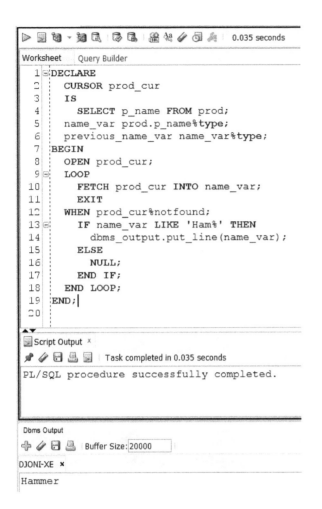

```
1  DECLARE
2     CURSOR prod_cur
3     IS
4       SELECT p_name FROM prod;
5     name_var prod.p_name%type;
6     previous_name_var name_var%type;
7  BEGIN
8     OPEN prod_cur;
9     LOOP
10      FETCH prod_cur INTO name_var;
11      EXIT
12    WHEN prod_cur%notfound;
13      IF name_var LIKE 'Ham%' THEN
14        dbms_output.put_line(name_var);
15      ELSE
16        NULL;
17      END IF;
18    END LOOP;
19  END;
20
```

Script Output ×

Task completed in 0.035 seconds

PL/SQL procedure successfully completed.

Dbms Output

Buffer Size: 20000

DJONI-XE ×

Hammer

Chapter 6: Creating Your Own Function

As a SQL user you should have used quite a number of SQL built-in functions.

- The AVG function we have used in many of the previous program examples is one of the built-in functions.

Using PL/SQL, you can create your own function.

```
CREATE FUNCTION less_avg(
    price NUMBER)
  RETURN CHAR
IS
  --DECLARE
  price_avg NUMBER;
BEGIN
  SELECT AVG(unit_price) INTO price_avg FROM prod ;
  IF price < price_avg THEN
    RETURN 'Y';
  ELSE
    RETURN 'N';
  END IF;
END;
```

- A stored function is a database object, hence you use a CREATE statement.
- We name the function as less_avg (less than average).
- Our function takes a parameter, the price. We will use the function to test if a price (the parameter) is less (or not) than the average of the unit prices of the products.
- A function, when used, returns a value; hence, you must specify the RETURN on the CREATE statement after the name and parameter.
  - As opposed to a function, a procedure when executed does some something (actions)
- The declaration part no longer needs the DECLARE reserved word; it is commented in the example below.
- When you execute the CREATE FUNCTION statement, the program is compiled and stored in the database as indicated by the message on the Script Output; you have not run the program yet. See next section: Using Stored Function.

```
Worksheet    Query Builder
  1 ⊟ CREATE FUNCTION less_avg(
  2       price NUMBER)
  3     RETURN CHAR
  4   IS
  5     --DECLARE
  6     price_avg NUMBER;
  7   BEGIN
  8       SELECT AVG(unit_price) INTO price_avg FROM prod ;
  9 ⊟   IF price < price_avg THEN
 10         RETURN 'Y';
 11     ELSE
 12         RETURN 'N';
 13     END IF;
 14   END;
 15
```

Script Output ×

📌 ✓ 💾 🖨 🖹   Task completed in 0.032 seconds

Function LESS_AVG compiled

Using Stored Function

You use a stored function in SQL statement the same way you use the built-in functions.

- Here is an example SQL statement in which we use our *less_avg* function.

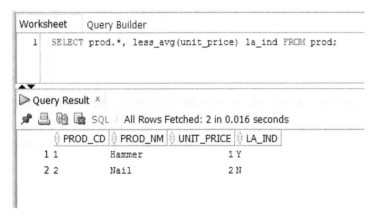

```
Worksheet    Query Builder
  1   SELECT prod.*, less_avg(unit_price) la_ind FROM prod;
```

▷ Query Result ×

📌 💾 🖺 🖺 SQL   All Rows Fetched: 2 in 0.016 seconds

	PROD_CD	PROD_NM	UNIT_PRICE	LA_IND
1	1	Hammer	1	Y
2	2	Nail	2	N

Securing and Sharing Stored Function

Similar to procedure, to secure and share a function, apply the GRANT.

Appendix: Installing SQL Developer and DB Express

The Appendix guides you to get and install the Oracle Data Base Express Edition and SQL Developer.

Database Express Edition

Go to http://www.oracle.com/technetwork/indexes/downloads/index.html

Locate and download the Windows version of the Oracle Database Express Edition (XE). You will be requested to accept the license agreement. If you don't have one, create an account; it's free.

Unzip the downloaded file to a folder in your local drive, and then, double-click the setup.exe file.

You will see the Welcome window.

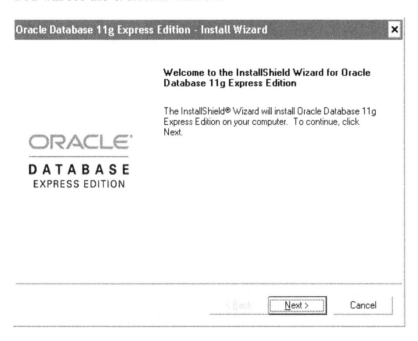

Click the Next> button, accept the agreement on the License Agreement window, and then click the Next> button again.

The next window is the "Choose Destination Location" window.

Accept the destination folder shown, or click the Browse button to choose a different folder for your installation, and then click the Next> button.

On the prompt for port numbers, accept the defaults, and then click the Next> button.

On the Passwords window, enter a password of your choice and confirm it, and then click the Next> button. The SYS and SYSTEM accounts created during this installation are for the database operation and administration, respectively. Note the password; you will use the SYSTEM account and its password for creating your own account, which you use for trying the examples.

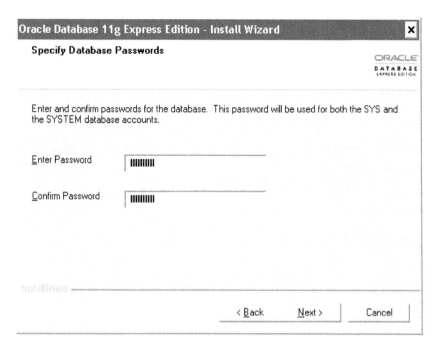

The Summary window will be displayed. Click Install.

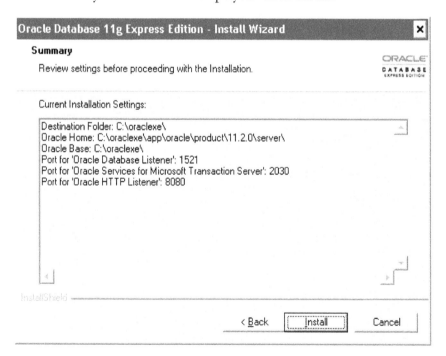

Finally, when the Installation Completion window appears, click the Finish button.

Your Oracle Database XE is now installed.

SQL Developer

SQL Developer is optional to try the book examples. Instead of using SQL Developer, you can run DDL on SQL*Plus for example. But I recommend using the GUI of the SQL Developer.

Go to http://www.oracle.com/technetwork/indexes/downloads/index.html

Locate and download the SQL Developer. You will be requested to accept the license agreement. If you don't have one, create an account; it's free.

Unzip the downloaded file to a folder of your preference. Note the folder name and its location; you will need to know them to start your SQL Developer.

When the unzipping is completed, look for the sqldeveloper.exe file.

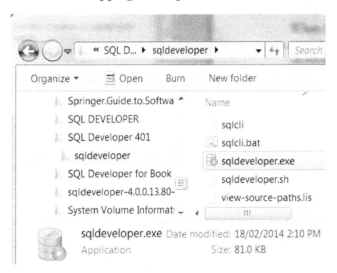

You start SQL Developer by opening (double-clicking) this file.

You might want to create a short-cut on your Desktop.

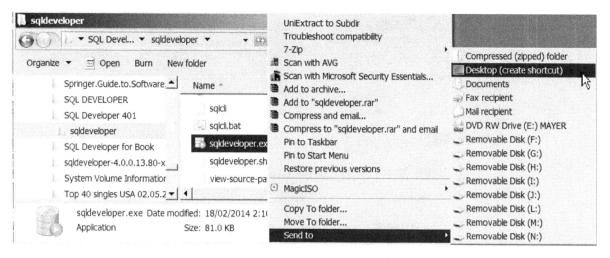

You can then start your SQL Developer by double-clicking the short-cut.

Your initial screen should look like the following. If you don't want to see the Start Page tab the next time you start SQL Developer, un-check the *Show on Startup* box at the bottom left side of the screen.

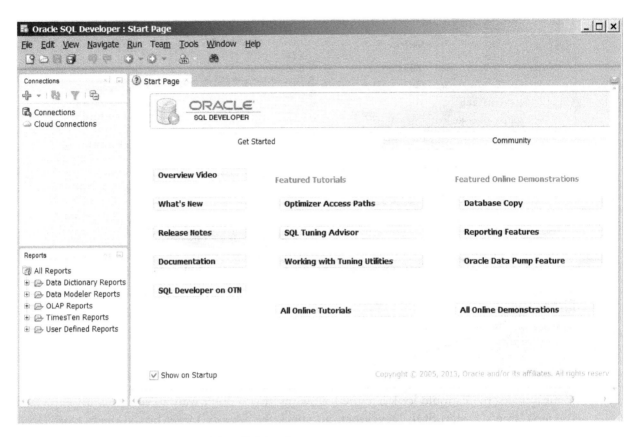

For now, close the Start Page tab by clicking its x.

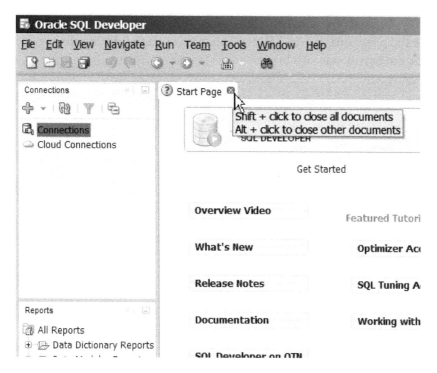

Creating Connection

To work with a database from SQL Developer, you need to have a connection.

A connection is specific to an account. As we will use the SYSTEM account to create your own account, you first have to create a connection for the SYSTEM account.

To create a connection, right-click the Connection folder.

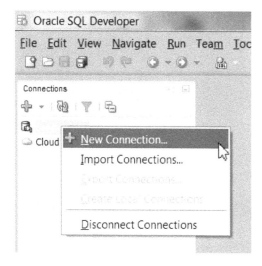

On the New/Select Database Connection window, enter a Connection Name and Username as shown. The Password is the password of SYSTEM account you entered during the Oracle database installation. Check the Save Password box.

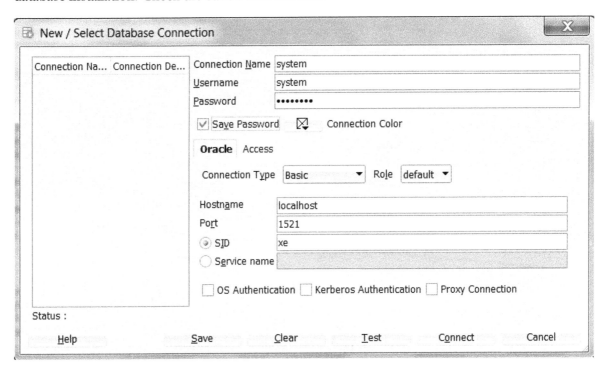

When you click the Connect button, the *system* connection you have just created should be available on the Connection Navigator.

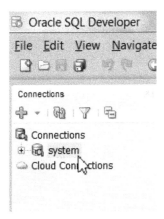

A Worksheet is opened for the system connection. The Worksheet is where you type in source codes.

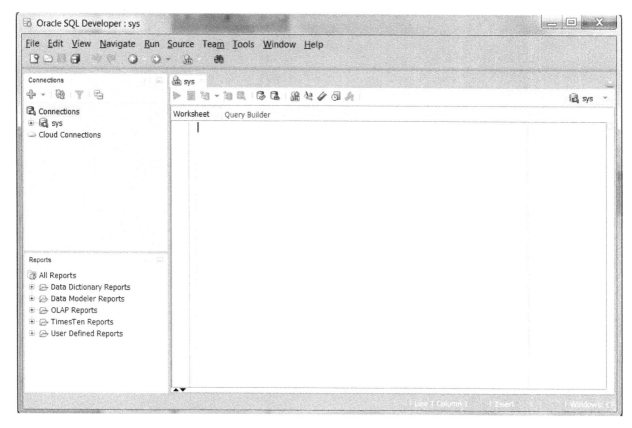

Creating Database Account

You will use your own database account (user) to try the book examples.

To create a new account, expand the system connection and locate the Other Users folder at the bottom of the folder tree.

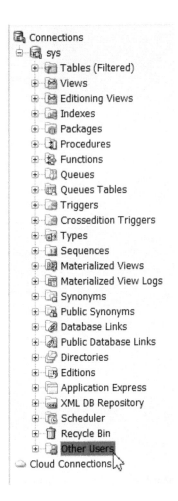

Right click and select Create User.

Enter a User Name of your choice, a password and its confirmation, and then click the Apply button. You should get a successful pop-up window; close it.

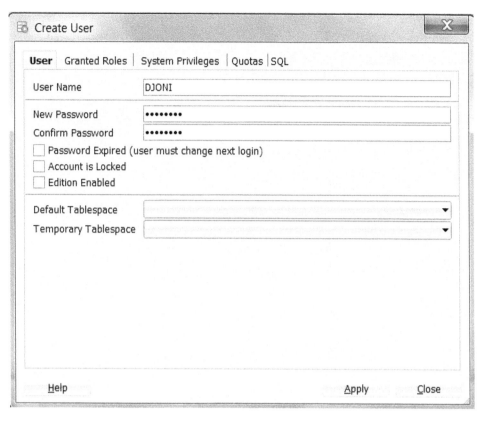

On the Granted Roles tab, click Grant All, Admin All and Default All buttons; then click the Apply button. Close the successful window and the Edit User as well.

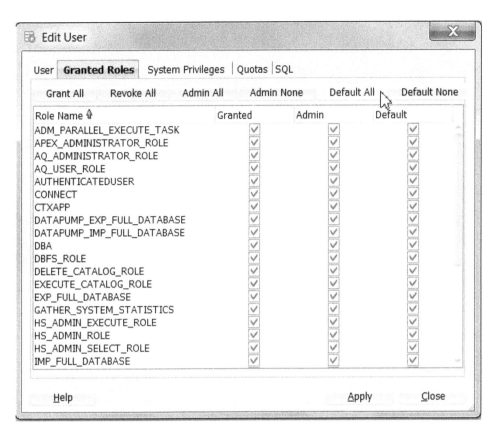

Creating Your Connection

Similar to when you created system connection earlier, now create a connection for your account.

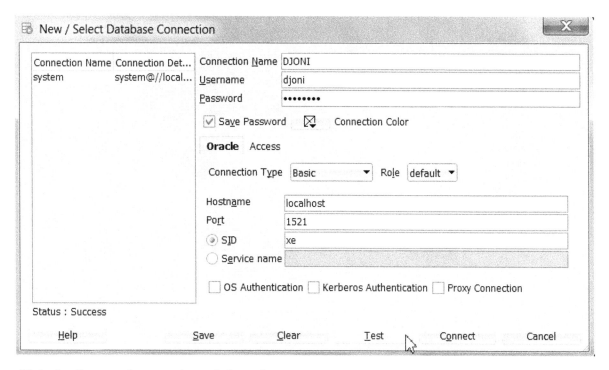

Click the Connect button. A worksheet for your connection is opened (which is *DJONI* in my case).

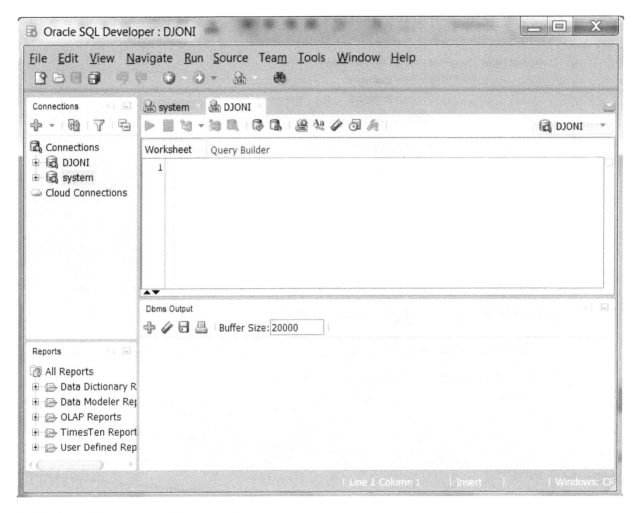

Deleting the *system* Connection

Delete the *system* connection, making sure you don't use this account mistakenly. Click Yes when you are prompted to confirm the deletion. Your SQL Developer is now set.

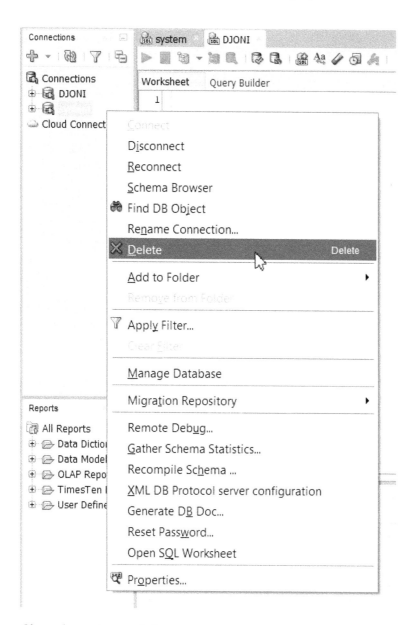

Close the *system* worksheet.

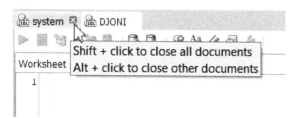

Index

www.ingramcontent.com/pod-product-compliance
Lightning Source LLC
Chambersburg PA
CBHW060509060326
40689CB00020B/4683